THE MAYBERRY CHRONICLES

poems by

Ed Sawyer

Finishing Line Press
Georgetown, Kentucky

THE MAYBERRY CHRONICLES

Copyright © 2021 by Gustavo Pérez Firmat
ISBN 978-1-64662-507-9 First Edition
All rights reserved under International and Pan-American Copyright Conventions. No part of this book may be reproduced in any manner whatsoever without written permission from the publisher, except in the case of brief quotations embodied in critical articles and reviews.

ACKNOWLEDGMENTS

Grateful acknowledgement is made to *County Lines,* in which "Inside Andy Taylor" first appeared.

Publisher: Leah Huete de Maines

Editor: Christen Kincaid

Cover Art: Mayberry street scene photo courtesy of Marc Wannamaker, Bison Archives; photo design by Brady Lambert, Southeastern Camera.

Author Photo: Courtesy of Mary Anne Pérez

Cover Design: Elizabeth Maines McCleavy

Printed in the USA on acid-free paper.
Order online: www.finishinglinepress.com
            also available on amazon.com

Author inquiries and mail orders:
Finishing Line Press
P. O. Box 1626
Georgetown, Kentucky 40324
U. S. A.

Table of Contents

A Prologue by Ed Sawyer, "The Stranger in Town" 1
Inside Andy 2
Barney Flies Off the Handle 3
Floyd in the Driver's Seat 4
Otis Comes Clean 5
Miss Ellie Speaks Out 6
Barney Recants 7
Thelma Lou Stands by Her Man 8
Aunt Bee Lusts after the Butter and Egg Man 9
Briscoe Feels the Pain of Rejection 10
Gomer Comes Out of the Closet 11
The Taylors' Neighbor Complains 12
Opie's Pet Turtle Talks 12
Leon Says Something 12
The Fun Girls Explain What Happened 13
The Squad Car Takes a Day Off 14
The Loaded Goat Unloads 15
Judd and Asa Shoot the Breeze In Front of the Courthouse 16
Warren Ferguson Vents 17
The Pounded Steak at Morelli's 18
Sharon DeSpain Dishes the Dirt 19
Emmett Clark Apologizes 20
Clara Clears Up the Confusion 21
Aunt Bee Takes another Turn 22
The Mirror in Floyd's Babershop Looks Back 23
Mr. Schwump Tells All 24
The Man in a Hurry Stops to Think 25
Malcolm Merriweather Takes His Leave 26

Ernest T. Bass Soliloquizes 27
Helen Makes a Night of It 28
A Fish Out Of Water 29
Goober's Secret 30
Opie Reminisces 31
Dialogue Between a Rock and a Hard Place 32
Sarah Puts Down the Phone 33
Howard Sprague Wants Out 34
A Valediction by Reverend Tucker of All Souls Church 35
A Postscript by Ed Sawyer 36

A Prologue By Ed Sawyer, "The Stranger in Town"

I never got to know them well enough. I met them, years ago now, when they were little more than moving shadows. Afterwards I lived with them, or they with me, for months at a time, and I never did understand them as well as I would have liked. Mayberrians are not easy to know. Friendly but not familiar, they show you what they intend to show you; then they leave or turn away and you're left standing there, hand or arms outstretched, with nothing in your grasp but dead air.

I wanted more. I wanted intimacy, the kind that exists only among people who can read one another's minds. I dreamed about looking inside them, fleshing out the shadows. Finally they let me.

Inside Andy

I'll tell you what it is about fishing.
It's not about the fish; it's about the water.
It must be I've an island inside me
because when I'm on that lake, no one around
but my boy, both of us surrrounded by water,
it doesn't matter if we catch anything or not.

The man with the badge and the uniform
isn't me. The fisherman isn't me. The friend
and the boyfriend isn't me. The nephew isn't me.
The good neighbor and good guy isn't me.
Who I am is a man who loves to sit in a row boat
with his son, in the middle of a clear lake, doing nothing.
Like I said, there must be an island inside me.

Barney Flies Off the Handle

So what if he's taller and better-looking.
So what if he pretends that he's cleaning a rifle
while I pace. Don't you think I don't notice.
Sometimes I get tired too, tired of his rifles
and his aunt and that kid, so cute
that when he walks into the courthouse and says,
"Hi, Paw," I want to go into the back room
and barf. And something else he doesn't know,
that know-it-all, his girlfriend Helen,
the pudgy face that launched
a thousand trips to Myers Lake,
that one, she's a good one too. Andy should ask
the Darling boys about her. For once
they wouldn't be able to keep their mouths shut.

Floyd in the Driver's Seat

Ah, yes. It looks like me driving, doesn't it?
Pulling into the gas station to check out
the girl attendant in blue jeans?
Well, it's not. How can I drive when I can't
grip a comb? I faked it for years.
Even at the beginning, before the stroke,
did you ever see me actually snip a lock of hair,
cut a cowlick, fix Barney's sideburns?
No, it was all fake, all acting. The less I moved,
the more I acted. It was all in my face, you see.
It never stopped moving. Even the twitch was faked.
And then they said I had retired and moved away.
Don't you believe it. The third stroke killed me.
No amount of acting could have made up for that.

Otis Comes Clean

Sure I'm a drunk, and it's true that once
I fell off a wall sideways. But you haven't heard
the half of it. It's about my ties.
Remember? Even in black-and-white
they burst with color. I roamed
the state looking for them, short and wide
and striped like the rainbow.
When I couldn't find any, I drank.
It wasn't the missus or the glue factory
or not having friends. Get me a new tie,
short and wide and striped like the rainbow,
and I don't need a wife, a job, or friends.
This is what no one understands,
that it was always about my ties.

Miss Ellie Speaks Out

It was good while it lasted
but it didn't.
What spoiled it was the election.
Andy didn't like it at first,
then he liked it when I won,
but later, when I started going
to the Council meetings
instead of skipping stones
in the lake or taking in a show,
that's when the friction began.
He didn't say much, he never
said much, but things changed.
And if there was one thing he hated,
it was change. Routine was his
life. I'm told that he had
other sweethearts after me
and married a school teacher.
For her sake, I hope she doesn't
run for the school board.

Barney Recants

It wasn't the way I said, not exactly.
You know me, I stretch the truth
a little. I didn't mean anything by it.
Andy is like a brother to me,
and Opie and Aunt Bee are my family too,
and Helen, she's Thel's best friend.
I was just blowing off steam, like other times.

Like Andy says I'm proud.
I do get tired, fed up, but with myself,
with who I want to be and who I'm not.
I'm not reliable or fearless or eagle-eyed.
The truth, Juanita had no use for me.
The truth, I failed as a detective in Raleigh.

I'm Barney Fife, a small man
with big plans that never come true.

Thelma Lou Stands by Her Man

No, he's not Andy.
And he's not like Howard
or the boys in the barbershop either.
I know what you see: the sniffing,
the duck waddle, the bullet in the pocket.
Yes, he's stingy and he can't sing a note.
When he gets frisky, his bug-eyes pop out
and his hair stands on end.

I know all that, but I see more.
I see more than he sees himself.
Give me a choice, Andy or Barney,
the town's most eligible bachelor or its laughing stock,
and it's Barney every time.

My Barney, not good enough
in every way but one: I love him.

Aunt Bee Lusts after the Butter and Egg Man

It wasn't a fib at all.
As usual, the writers got it wrong.
Just because I never married,
it doesn't mean I haven't… you know…
My, Clara could tell you some stories
about Normal School. I never slept
in the same bed twice.
Honey Bee, that's what they called me.

And then I got stuck in this town
with nothing to do except bake pies
and change the sheets. And I hate to bake!
You want to know why you never saw
Andy's bedroom? Or the bathrooms?
Because they were filthy, that's why.
I refuse to clean up after a grown man.

So when Orville, dear sweet Orville,
the butter and egg man from Mt. Pilot,
when he started dropping by twice a week,
strolling into the kitchen
with the swagger of a butter and egg man,
I became the honey.
The writers, poor souls, called him
"Aunt Bee's Invisible Beau."
Fiddlesticks! Beautiful he certainly was
and most visible. Those writers,
they had no idea what went on in Mayberry.

Briscoe Darling Feels the Pain of Rejection

I'm not much for talking, but you asked. We Darlings are a proud family and we don't take to being spurned. First it was my Charlene, a sweet girl who sings like a bird and cooks the tastiest catfish stew this side of the mountains. She's got a mind of her own, and it was set on the Sheriff, but he shuns her. Then I go a-courting Miss Bee and she wants no part of me. That wasn't the worst of it. When Andelina was born, I ride into town fixing to betroth her to the Sheriff's boy. Little Andelina, she's the joy of this granddaddy's heart. But they didn't cotton to that neither, even with the dowry, a cow and two acres of side hill with boulders on it, large ones. Sheriff Taylor thinks he tricked me all three times, that it was us that backed out, but I saw through that rider in the night trick, like I saw through the disappearing ink and the other things. No, if the Taylors didn't jump at the chance to tie their fortunes to the Darlings, I wasn't going to insist on it. Still and all, Sheriff's a good man—a little too nervous maybe—and he does some mighty fine pickin'. As I told him one time, that haircut of his may be city-style, but his heart was shaped in a bowl. Who knows, could be one day me and the Sheriff will be sittin' in my cabin, scrubbin' one on, while little Darlings, or little Taylors, run up and down that hill.

Gomer Comes Out of the Closet

They knew.
They all knew.
That's why they shipped me off
to the Marines. "It'll make a man of him,"
they whispered. But don't think I minded.
The only thing I missed was the purple tie
with the acorns on it. Not the gas station.
Not the choir. Not the dances. Not Andy and Barney.
(Well, I did miss Andy, a little, after a while…)

But I would have left anyway.
Wally's Service was not for me.
I wanted more.
Whether they liked it or not,
I was going to become the man I was.

The Taylors' Neighbor Complains

Will those people next door
stop singing and turn off the porch light,
so that the rest of us can sleep?

Opie's Pet Turtle Talks

If you ask me, they were a strange bunch.
At night, I could hear Aunt Bee in her room
and Andy in his, talking. To whom, I have no idea.
They talked and talked and then it was silent.
All I ever got to eat was left-over collards.

Leon Says Something

I wanted to scream,
but Opie wouldn't let me.

The Fun Girls Explain What Happened

—I'm Daphne.
—I'm Skippy.
—I'm the one with the throaty voice.
—I'm the cute one.
—I'm Andy's girl.
—I'm Bernie's.
—The name's Barney.
—I like Bernie better.
—Andy's a doll.
—Bernie's a scream.
—We dated them twice.
—Three times.
—We dropped them.
—Poor Bernie, it broke his little heart.
—They wouldn't take us anywhere.
—I love the Gigolo Club!
—And seeing other women on the side.
—Floozies.
—Dumb and dumber.
—Serves them right.
—They won't be missed.
—(*Together, with gusto*) We are the Fun Girls!

The Squad Car Takes a Day Off

They drove me crazy, those two.
It wasn't enough that I had to chase
god-knows-who down dirt roads or
up Turner's Grade. It wasn't enough
that I carried groceries for Aunt Bee,
Emma Brand and every other old lady
in town. It wasn't enough that come
Founder's Day I had to follow, lights
flashing, our so-called band playing something
that sounded nothing like "Stars and Stripes."
No, even that wasn't enough. Two words:
Myers Lake. No, make it four: Myers Lake,
Duck Pond. I don't know where that sheriff,
who couldn't set a speed trap if his life
depended on it, or his deputy, whose foot
barely reached my accelerator, got the idea
I was made for what they called "parking."
I will admit that the girls were cute
but this is not what Henry Ford had in mind.
Oh, if only I'd been around for *Highway Patrol*.

The Loaded Goat Unloads

I wanna tell you, some people have no feelings
for animals. First they make me eat dynamite,
then they throw me in jail, and then they walk me out of town
so that I can explode all by myself. "Go blooey,"
as that idiot Barney put it. Well, I'll tell you what.
I'm not an old goat for nothing. After they left me,
I snuck back into the armory. And here I am,
a dynamite stick clenched between my teeth, waiting…

Judd and Asa Shoot the Breeze In Front of the Courthouse

—I was asleep.
—Asleep? (*Begins whittling.*)
—Yes, when it happened.
—When what happened?
—The bank.
—The bank?
—That one. (*Points down the street.*)
—I know. You were asleep and robbers cleaned it out… Don't much matter, though. (*Continues to whittle.*)
—No, I guess it don't.
—If it wasn't the bank, would have been something else. Peculiar things been going on ever since that young'un got into the sheriffin' business.
—It's because of Barney, if you ask me. Even as a boy he was different.
—Last week I'm going to Walker's for some sleep powder and what do I see? (*Stops whittling.*)
—How should I know what you saw? You're an old fool, you know that? You're so blind you can't see anything anyway.
—Don't old fool me, you geezer. Wanna know what I saw or not?
—Don't much matter.
—I saw Otis Campbell riding a cow into town. (*Resumes whittling.*)
—He says it was a horse.
—Well, it was a cow.
—If you didn't like it, you could've limped over on that gimpy leg of yours, grabbed the cow by the horns…
—Cows don't have horns. You *are* a fool.
—Don't much matter if they do or don't. I say they do. But you could've stopped him.
—Andy stopped him.
—Andy? (*Puts down the penknife.*)
—Now you're interested?

Warren Ferguson Vents

Boy, was I glad to be out of there!
Getting used to the South was hard enough
but getting Andy to accept me was impossible,
even if I *was* Floyd's nephew.
Barney's leaving hit Andy real hard,
almost like a betrayal, and he just wasn't himself.
After a week of his mood swings,
I began to dread showing up at the courthouse.
Sure, sometimes I messed up, but so did Barney.
The only reason I stayed was my uncle,
to be near him. I kept hoping Andy would calm down,
kept hoping that he'd warm up to me,
but the writers decided to write me out.
If Andy put them up to it, he did both of us a favor.

The Pounded Steak at Morelli's

Ouch!

Sharon DeSpain Dishes the Dirt

Rumor has it
Andy and I
were highschool
sweethearts.
Not quite.
I liked him
well enough
but he bored me.
I wanted
to get romantic.
He wanted
to play his guitar.
If I didn't hear about
that little brown church
in the vale
a dozen times,
I didn't hear about it
once. As I said,
he was a nice boy,
handsome, well-groomed,
a good appetite,
but he had no life.

Emmet Clark Apologizes

I took over his place, but I couldn't replace him.
Honey Tewilliger, Hollis Putney,
Agnes Drumhiller, Bobby Gribble,
Fluffy Johnson—they're not even names
to me, but Floyd knew all about them.
That's why everyone went to the barbershop,
not the haircuts but the stories.
My shelves are stacked with fans
that don't fan and toasters that don't toast.
Floyd's barbershop was filled with stories,
stories with the scent of witch hazel.
Some fix-it man I am.

Clara Clears Up the Confusion

Yes, I deserved the Grand Prize. Bee was never very good with flowers. Her talents lie elsewhere, if I may say so. She thinks I'm uppity about it, but I've always had a special knack for roses. Clorinated water, that's my secret. Brings out the bloom like nothing can. That and pest control, of course. Spray, spray, spray! I did say at the garden show that her Pink Ecstasy was superior to my Snow Valley White, but I was lying—a Valley White lie, if you wish. Bee had so set her heart on winning, that I let her think she had, just this once. Next year, I won't be so generous, Pink Ecstasy or no Pink Ecstasy.

Aunt Bee Takes another Turn

Frankly I never saw myself as "the new housekeeper"
even though that's what the writers called me.
I don't mean to pick on the writing but—really!
I wasn't a housekeeper and I wasn't new.
I raised Andy from the time he was a little boy
to the day he got married. From my arms to his wife's.
That's why everybody in town knew me.
Did you ever hear Barney or Floyd or anyone
else ask who I was? Of course not.
I waited and waited for that Rose woman to leave—
she was the housekeeper—dishes and dirt,
dirt and dishes, that's what she did. As soon
as she left, I came back to Mayberry,
the only place I've ever felt at home. And yes,
Opie had become attached to the housekeeper
but it didn't take him long to forget her, did it?
After that first day, he never mentioned the name again.
Had the writers asked me, I would have told them
the correct title for the first episode: Aunt Bee's Homecoming.

The Mirror in Floyd's Barbershop Looks Back

After watching them look into me all those years,
I grew fond of them. And so I'd touch up their reflections.
When Barney looked at me, he saw Sinatra.
When Goober looked at me, he saw Cary Grant.
When Gomer looked at me, he saw Jim Nabors.
When Otis looked at me, he looked dapper.
When Mayor Pike looked at me, he stopped lisping.
When Mayor Stoner looked at me, he was the governor.
When Andy looked at me, he saw Opie.
When Opie looked at me, he saw his Paw.
The only one who didn't need touching up was Floyd.
As long as he could see himself, he was happy.

Mr. Schwump Tells All

I'm Augustus Schwump.
Like an overgrown child, seen and not heard.
I've caught your eye many times—in church, at the Garden
Club, at Miss Wiley's parties. You've seen me dancing
and at a picnic or two. Where you've never seen me
is at the lake, fishing, because I can't swim.
Or at the barbershop, because I wear a toupée.
You know my face (droopy), my taste in suits (conservative)
and women (young), but you don't know anything else about me.
Unlike most of my town friends, I keep my own counsel.

But if you walk to the end of Main Street, past the hardware store,
the bank, the hotel, you will come upon a used car lot.
Maybe you haven't noticed it, but it's right there,
across from the cemetery: Schwump Auto Sales.
I'm proud to say that almost every car in Mayberry
drove away from my lot. I sold Otis his first (and last) car.
Mayors Stoner and Pike, the Tuckers, the Simses, the Farleys,
the Clarks, Mr. Masters, Howard Sprague (a tough sale)—all customers
of mine. Something else you may not be aware of:
For twenty years I was the driving instructor at Mayberry Union High.
What little they know about cars, Andy and Barney learned from me.

I never married though I came close, once.
For the rest, I can't complain. It's been a good life.
Few peaks, but fewer valleys.
Now that you know what there is to know
about me, you'll never hear from me again.

The Man in a Hurry Stops to Think

The car broke down.
It changed my life.

Malcolm Merriweather Takes His Leave

I kept going back until I couldn't go back any longer. By my last visit I knew it was impossible. Not because they talked and dressed unlike me, of course, or because I had been a gentleman's gentleman back home, an occupation unknown in Mayberry. The townspeople were gracious to me, exceedingly (all save one, that wild man, but he disappeared into the mountains). The Sheriff asked me to stay, settle down, join the Lodge, go crow shooting, but I couldn't. I didn't belong there, you see. I could no more become a Mayberrian than they could become Englishmen. For two years I biked around their country, all my possessions in a satchel, looking for a place to begin again. When I find it, a congenial place, quiet, full of kind people, I cannot stop thinking about Eckmondwight. It's strange, isn't it, how little we take to transplanting.

Ernest T. Bass Soliloquizes

Don't tell me you believe the nonsense
about me slinging rocks and jumping up
and down like a mad monkey
with the name of a fish.
I'm not Ernest nor am I Bass. I'm the T.
T as in Technical. T as in Twilight.
And I knew her name wasn't Romeena,
but it wasn't Ramona either. It was Joan.

The one thing they got right was Charlene,
Charlene Darling: my love. When she sang
"Salty Dog" I trembled like a T in the wind.
She pranced around, kicking up her feet
and lifting up her skirt, and it made me
crazy. That's what got me rhyming. Bottled up
libido spilling in song. The rest was Hollywood
foolery, like the time I wanted to marry Barney in drag.
(*You* think *I* couldn't tell? Couldn't *you*?)

That's the thing about TV shows,
they turn you into someone you're not, for laughs.
Look at me, just look, and you'll see the T.

Helen Makes a Night of It

I thought he would never propose!
We spent YEARS going together
and it was always, "The time's not right."
I don't know what time he was waiting for
because I wasn't getting any younger and neither was he.
When I left Kansas I'd had my fill of cornfed Casanovas.
I'd been engaged, dumped, engaged again, dumped once more.
I wanted steady. I wanted predictable. I wanted dull!
Andy fit the bill. So I traded my jeans and sweaters
for slacks so slack I could have fit two of me in them.
And I changed my name. Yes, I did. —Surprised?
Well, you shouldn't be. Do I look like a "Crump" to you?
I figured "DeAngelis" was a little too ethnic for Mayberry,
maybe ok for a restaurant but a stretch for Opie's teacher.
"Crump" is what Andy wanted, and "Crump" is what he got.
Until our wedding night, that is.

A Fish Out Of Water

They call me Old Sam.
Only God knows why.
I'm old but I'm not a Sam.

I'm a Silver Carp
(indexed Carp, Silver),
the biggest fish in the lake.

For longer than I care
to remember, they've
been trying to snag me.

Floyd, the eternal optimist.
Barney, the gadget man.
Andy, who thinks it's all

in how you bait the hook.
(News for Andy: I don't
eat worms.) Who I wasn't

prepared for was Howard,
the first timer. My taste
for adventure betrayed me.

He lured me with potato salad.
I thought I would gobble
and run, but before I'd had

a good gulp, I was gasping
for air. Dear Howard.
His conscience wouldn't

let him fry me. He put me
in an aquarium in Raleigh
but I pined for Mayberry.

So back into the lake I went,
the one Silver Carp in a town
teeming with queer fish.

Goober's Secret

They made me wear that damned hat. I hated it.
When no one was watching I'd stomp
on it, but the worse it looked the better
they liked it, Andy and the others.
I wanted to style, wear double-breasted suits,
two-toned shoes, just like Cary.
I wanted to be a star. But to them I was Goober
the goofy gas jockey. It depressed the hell out of me.
Once I fell in love and it lasted all of twenty minutes.
Always Goober the goof, good for a gag or two.
What did those people know about love, about longing,
about loneliness? Nothing, that's what.
I'm a dreamer. No one ever dreamed in Mayberry.

Opie Reminisces

It's hard to believe I was that boy.
All that hair! But I suppose growing up
in Mayberry wasn't so different
from growing up anywhere else.
We had our widows, our creepy
old men, the complement of bratty kids.
My Dad (he became "Paw" for your benefit)
never seemed to do much. Sing in the choir.
Fish at the lake. Strum his guitar.
And work. That was about it.
When I moved away he stopped fishing,
he said, because he missed me too much.
I could never tell what was going on inside him.
I still can't.

Aunt Bee, God bless her, she was a free spirit.
Every week she cooked up a new idea:
a car, a restaurant, flying lessons, commercials,
a trip to Mexico. She hatched more schemes than Barney,
but I don't know how happy she was, really.
Even as a kid I sensed that something was off.
Remember the time we all thought Dad
was getting married and she had Dad's room
redecorated with flowered wallpaper and a canopied bed?
Of course Dad wasn't getting married. So instead
he traded bedrooms with Bee. She was so thrilled
it was like she was getting married. I believe
Aunt Bee minded being single far more than Dad.

As for me, you wouldn't recognize me,
though I really haven't changed much.
I still can't dance or carry a tune.
After finishing at Carolina, I became a teacher,
like Helen, and moved out of state.
Sometimes I still wake up dreaming
about Winkin, Blinkin and Nod, the baby birds.
I didn't have a mother either, maybe
that's why I felt so bad about what happened,
even if it *was* an accident. That was the last time
I ever used my slingshot.

Dialogue Between a Rock and a Hard Place

—I've seen them walk by every week for years. The man always whistling the same tune. The boy always picking the same pebble, flinging it with the same motion, and landing it in the same spot in the water. It was uncanny.
—I've never seen them, though I've heard them often enough.
—I know what you mean.
—They sure love to talk, those people. About nothing. Not even about the weather. It's always, "Know what I'm gonna do?" "What?" "I'm gonna go down to the gas station and get me a bottle of pop." Every night. Same f-ing gas station, same f-ing bottle of pop.
—You'd think nothing ever happened to them, the way they act.
—I used to think it was easy being a hard place, but my life is nothing compared to theirs.
—Almost makes you wish you'd been born human, doesn't it?
—Nah.

Sarah Puts Down the Phone

You've never seen me
and you've never heard me,
but I know everything.
I've been sitting at this switchboard,
earphones around my head like a halo,
for forty years, maybe longer.
Nothing gets past me.
I was right here when Andy was born
and the year his ma and his daddy passed, poor child;
when Barney ran away and everyone thought he was dead
(I found him in Siler City); when the bank was robbed;
when the gypsies came through; when Floyd and his wife
quarreled for months on end. —Why?
Ask the manicurist, if you can find her.
But don't believe everything you hear. I don't.
I listen, keep my mouth shut, and make connections.

Howard Sprague Wants Out

I was Floyd's landlord,
but you know me better
as the County Clerk,
the only job I've ever had.

Millie was my girl, *my*
girl, until Sam Jones,
that parvenu, stole her
from me. Mama's boy,

he called me. And still
I had to sit in the Town
Council meetings with him.
I never got over it.

Things were so different
when Andy was around.
That's when Mayberry
was Mayberry, the friendly

town. Now I walk along
Main Street and don't know
half the faces. It's not
my town anymore. It's theirs.

A Valediction By Reverend Tucker Of All Souls Church

I never worried about their souls, to tell you the truth, because I doubt that anybody ever sinned. Big sins, I mean. Peccadilloes, of course, we had our share: murmuring, a stray curse now and then, and more than little gluttony come Founder's Day. Nothing that a stretch of clean living did not wash away. Looking at them from the pulpit, I thought to myself: if only those without sin can cast the first stone, everyone in my congregation could have been like Ernest T. Bass, who started throwing rocks before he could walk. (I know, I baptized him.)

Their one bad habit was hostility to outsiders. On many a Sabbath I preached that when Christ commanded us to love our neighbor, He didn't mean the folks across the street or at the church social. At times I thought I had gotten through to them, but for the most part they continued as they had always been: tolerant of one another but suspicious of every one else. I guess that's part of who they were. Their kingdom, Mayberry, was not of this world.

A Postscript by Ed Sawyer

Guess there's not much else to say.
The Reverend just about sums it up.
Appreciate it. Good bye.

The End of the Mayberry Chronicles

A writer and scholar, Cuban-born **Gustavo Pérez Firmat** is the author of many books of cultural and literary criticism, among them Life on the Hyphen, a study of Cuban American culture that was awarded the Eugene M. Kayden University Press National Book Award, and the memoir Next Year in Cuba, which was nominated for a Pulitzer Prize. His poems and stories have appeared in many magazines and anthologies, including *The Oxford Book of Caribbean Verse, Growing Up in the South, The Prentice Hall Anthology of Latino Literature,* and *The Vintage Book of Contemporary Cuban Literature.* His most recent books are the poetry collections *Sin lengua, deslenguado* and *Viejo Verde.* He is a fellow of the American Academy of Arts and Sciences and has been the recipient of fellowships from the National Endowment for the Humanities, the American Council of Learned Societies, and the John Simon Guggenheim Memorial Foundation. Newsweek included him among "100 Americans to watch for the 21st century" and Hispanic Business Magazine selected him as one of the "100 most influential Hispanics" in the United States. He teaches Spanish American literature at Columbia University, where he is the David Feinson Professor in the Humanities.

www.ingramcontent.com/pod-product-compliance
Lightning Source LLC
LaVergne TN
LVHW041558070426
835507LV00011B/1155